ATTENTION: BE CAREFUL WHEN CONDUCTING
ANY OF THE EXPERIMENTS FOUND IN THIS BOOK.
ALWAYS FOLLOW THE INSTRUCTIONS AND NEVER
DO ANYTHING WITHOUT ADULT SUPERVISION.

THE SUPER BOOK OF SCIENCE
© Vilhelm Anton Jonsson 2013

This English edition © Edda Publishing USA LLC. 2017 **EDDA USA**

Title of the original Icelandic edition: VÍSINDABÓK VILLA
Published by agreement with Forlagid Publishing, www.forlagid.is

Translation: Bjorg Arnadottir and Andrew Cauthery
Layout and drawings: Dagny Reykjalin and Gudrun Hilmisdottir
Cover design: Gassi, Dagny Reykjalin and Gudrun Hilmisdottir
Photo credits: "Fossilized dinosaur skull" (page 5) and "Dried walnuts" (page 21), courtesy of
Shutterstock.
Printed in Canada

Distributed by Macmillan

ISBN: 978-1-94078-770-1

www.eddausa.com

THE SUPER BOOK OF
SCIENCE

VILHELM ANTON JONSSON

EDDA USA

HI! LIKE EVERYONE ELSE, I HAVE A FAVORITE FOOD, A FAVORITE BAND, AND A FAVORITE SONG. BUT I ALSO HAVE A FAVORITE QUESTION, WHICH IS —

why?

This little question is incredibly useful. It's one of the most awesomely powerful things you can imagine. You see, if we ask WHY enough times we will discover the truth.

Some people call this nosiness and find it irritating. I couldn't disagree more. It is the most precious thing we've got, being curious and wanting to understand the world around us. Finding out why things are the way they are! If we don't understand things, we can't change them, and if we can't change them, we can't improve the world and our lives. Knowledge is incredibly precious, and being able to benefit from knowledge all starts from asking this simple question and being nosy about everything! So I'll start with myself. Why did I write this book?

Because there are so many things in the world that I find exciting and awesome. This book doesn't deal with all of them, and you won't be able to understand everything in the world once you've read it. But if it makes some boy or girl who reads it just a bit more curious and makes them more interested in science and makes them ask more often why things are the way they are, then my object has been achieved and I'll be happy. Someone will know and understand more than they did before, and the world we all inhabit will be a little bit better because it has gained a new scientist. So always ask — Why?

Vilhelm

CONTENTS

THE SUPER BOOK OF
SCIENCE

DINOSAURS

DINOSAURS RULED THE EARTH FOR MORE THAN 160 MILLION YEARS, UNTIL THEIR SUDDEN EXTINCTION MORE THAN 65 MILLION YEARS AGO.

Some of them were enormous, whereas others were no bigger than chickens. They ruled the sea, air and land.

NOW YOU SEE THEM, NOW YOU DON'T!

BUT THEN THEY BECAME EXTINCT. Just like that! Most scientists think that this was because of some terrible NATURAL DISASTER that happened over 65 million years ago. Either a METEOR crashed into the earth, whirling up so much dust that it blocked out the sun for years and years, or else there were some huge volcanic ERUPTIONS that had the same effect. When that happened, the earth became very cold. Dinosaurs were cold-blooded REPTILES that could not adapt to the cold.

GOOD FOR US

It was actually good for us that the dinosaurs became extinct, because all the little mammals that shared the earth with them were able to adapt to the cold and they then turned into … ta da! … US.

WHAT DO YOU WANT FOR DINNER?

Some dinosaurs were CARNIVORES and ate other animals. Others were HERBIVORES that ate grass and vegetation, and these were then sometimes eaten by the carnivores. The herbivores had a variety of clever weapons to defend themselves, such as SPIKES on their tails, HORNS on their heads, and SHIELDS surrounding their heads. Some of them were, actually, kind of like tanks.

THE KING OF THE DINOSAURS

The TYRANNOSAURUS REX was a massive predatory reptile. It could grow up to 45 feet long and 20 feet tall. It walked on its very strong hind legs, but its forepaws were small and feeble. It had a big head, about 4 feet long (roughly the height of a 6-year-old kid). They were also heavy, about 5 to 9 tons, which is about as much as a hundred adult humans. But it was still not the biggest dinosaur. The biggest ones were a lot bigger than the Tyrannosaurus Rex.

SUPERSAURUS

... WHOOPS!

THIS IS HOW INCREDIBLY SMALL A HUMAN WOULD LOOK STANDING NEXT TO THE SUPERSAURUS

It was incredibly big. It was a herbivore, so it wouldn't eat us but it might well accidentally tread on us and it would be kind of painful if it were to step on your toe.

THE BIGGEST ONES DIDN'T EAT MEAT

The biggest dinosaurs were not carnivores, they were herbivores. Most scientists think that the heaviest dinosaur was the BRACHIOSAURUS. It could weigh as much as 60 tons and be 80 feet long, the length of an average public swimming pool. But the SUPERSAURUS was even bigger! It could grow to 140 feet, nearly as long as two tennis courts! A little lighter than the Brachiosaurus, it weighed about 55 tons, which is the weight of about 1000 teenagers! To put it into context, the heaviest land animal on earth in our times, the African elephant, weighs a mere 8 tons.

TYRANNOSAURUS REX

A GENUINE TYRANNOSAURUS REX SKULL!

LIFE WOULDN'T BE MUCH FUN IF YOU COULDN'T DO EXPERIMENTS. NOR WOULD LIFE BE MUCH FUN IF YOU DIDN'T MAKE MISTAKES. THAT'S HOW KNOWLEDGE IS BORN. BUT WHILE MAKING A MISTAKE ONCE IS ACCIDENTAL, MAKING THE SAME MISTAKE TWICE IS JUST MESSING AROUND. WE DON'T ALL NEED TO RUN INTO A WALL TO FIGURE OUT THAT IT IS HARD. WE ALSO HAVE TO USE OUR BRAINS.

FLOATING EGG

If I were to put an egg into my mom's glass of water, two things would happen: She would get really mad and the egg would sink.

THIS IS WHAT YOU NEED:

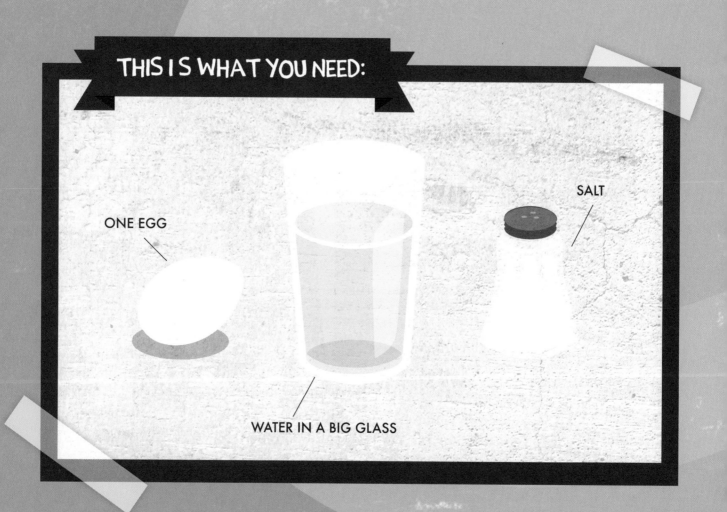

ONE EGG

WATER IN A BIG GLASS

SALT

1 Pour the water into the glass until it's half-full.

2 Stir loads of salt into the water, say about 6 tablespoons.

ABSOLUTELY DO NOT DRINK THIS WATER, IT WOULD MAKE YOU THROW UP ALL OVER THE PLACE!!

3 Now add more water until the glass is almost full. Do this VERY GENTLY so that the fresh water does NOT mix with the salt water already in the glass.

4 Gently put the egg into the water and watch what happens.

WHAT IS ACTUALLY GOING ON HERE?

NOW THE EGG SHOULD BE FLOATING IN THE CENTER OF THE GLASS.

Salt water is heavier than fresh water, and the heavier a liquid is, the more likely things are to float in it.

WHEN YOU LOWERED THE EGG INTO THE GLASS, IT SANK THROUGH THE FRESH WATER BUT STOPPED WHEN IT HIT THE SALT WATER.

But this will only happen if you've managed to pour the fresh water really gently into the glass.

ELECTRICITY

Electricity is incredibly useful. It is actually everywhere, and we use it for most of the things we do. We use it for computers, televisions, ovens, lights, radios, and most things, in fact. And yet electricity, as we know it from our daily lives, is not common in nature and it's almost INVISIBLE.

AN ELECTRONIC EXPRESSWAY

If we align a thousand million METAL ATOMS together, we create an expressway for electrons to travel along. A good example of this is electric cables, which transport electricity very well. We say that they CONDUCT it very well. But if, on the other hand, we stack together a thousand million different atoms that conduct electricity badly, we can make an impassable, bad road for the electrons. The rubber or plastic around the electric cable is a good example. It conducts very badly, which is good, because then we don't get a shock when we touch the cable.

AN ELECTRIC SHOWER

We can think about electricity like we think about water in a faucet. Behind every power outlet, there's a volume of electricity waiting to be turned on, so that it can flow into whatever is plugged into the outlet. The thing is that an ELECTRIC CURRENT is always seeking balance. There is a lot of voltage in the transmission lines in the walls, and the electricity wants to get out, to go to a lower voltage. An electric current will always go from the place where the voltage is high, to a place where the voltage is lower. That's why it wouldn't be very clever to touch a live electric fence or stick something into a power outlet that's not meant for it. It can actually be DEADLY DANGEROUS.

SOMETHING IS NEEDED TO KEEP THE WORLD TOGETHER!

ELECTRICAL POWER and **MAGNETIC FORCE** are closely related, and together these phenomena create what we call **ELECTROMAGNETISM**, which ... holds the universe together!
All **ELEMENTARY PARTICLES** have a certain electric charge that can be negative (electrons), positive (protons) or neutral (neutrons).
If there are equal numbers of protons and electrons in a material, it becomes neutral, meaning that it contains no electricity and we don't get a shock if we touch it.

WELL-COMBED SCIENCE!

When we comb dry hair with a plastic comb, electrons are transported from the atoms of the hair to those of the comb. The comb gets a negative charge while the hair becomes positive. If we tear a piece of toilet paper into small bits and bring the comb close to them, they will move around. That is electromagnetism pulling at them. It is the very same force that keeps the universe together.

Electricity actually holds everything together, from a single atom to the universe itself!

SUPER-ORANGE

Here's a simple question:

WHAT HAPPENS IF I PUT AN ORANGE IN A
BOWL FULL OF WATER?

You think so?
Let's try.

THIS IS WHAT YOU NEED:

AN ORANGE

A DEEP BOWL WITH
WATER IN IT

1. Put the orange into the bowl of water and see what happens!

2. Now peel the orange and put it back into the bowl.

WHAT IS ACTUALLY GOING ON HERE?

When you first put the orange in the bowl, I guess it floated. After you peeled it, I expect it sank.

WHAT SORT OF KUNG-FU VOODOO MAGIC IS GOING ON HERE?

The orange peel is full of little holes that contain air. This makes the orange lighter than the water, which is why it floats. When you peeled it, you actually took its life jacket off. In doing so, it became heavier than the water and sank to the bottom.

In other words, things have different densities. This is linked to mass, which I will be dealing with later in this book.

THE MOON

THE MOON HAS ALWAYS BEEN CONSPICUOUS. EVER SINCE THE FIRST HUMAN LOOKED UP TO THE SKY, THE MOON HAS BEEN THERE.

The **MOON** is the earth's satellite and is, in fact, its twin planet, about 240 **THOUSAND MILES AWAY**. THAT'S LIKE ONE HUNDRED JOURNEYS BETWEEN NEW YORK AND SEATTLE.

THE EARTH AND THE MOON pull at each other and revolve around each other and **THE SUN**. But the moon is gradually moving farther away from the earth, at a rate of about 1½ inches a year. It'll be a bit of a to-do in about two billion years, when the moon and the earth stop pulling at each other and the moon just glides away.

After the sun, the moon is the brightest object we can see in the sky.

THE MOON HAS ALWAYS FASCINATED US — IN FACT WE HAVE SENT MORE THAN 70 SPACECRAFT UP THERE TO STUDY IT.

The moon has a big influence on the earth. It controls the tides, for example, by pulling at the ocean when it's at its closest to earth.

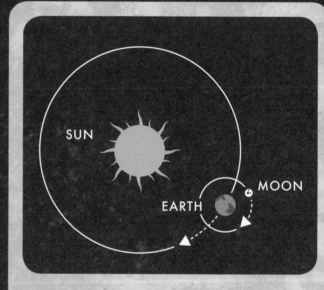

HERE WE SEE THE EARTH ON ITS COURSE AROUND THE SUN, AND THE MOON ON ITS COURSE AROUND THE EARTH.

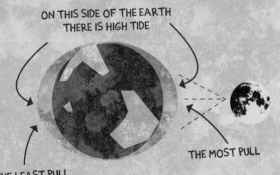

ON THIS SIDE OF THE EARTH
THERE IS HIGH TIDE

THE MOST PULL

THE LEAST PULL

THE MOON CONTROLS THE TIDES,
BOTH HIGH TIDE AND LOW TIDE.

Where the moon is closest to earth, its gravitational force pulls the sea, causing high tide. At the same time, high tide will be in the places that are farthest from the moon, on the exact opposite side of the globe. Here, the moon's gravitational force is at its weakest so it cannot pull at the sea.

SOMEWHERE ON THE MOON
THERE'S A PHOTOGRAPH!
In 1972, Charles Duke traveled to the moon on the space shuttle Apollo 16, and left a photograph of his family behind.

But a lunar month, the time it takes the moon to go from almost nothing (new moon) to full, and then back to nearly nothing, is 29 and a half days, so a little less than our calendar month.

PLATEAUS AND OCEANS

When we look at the moon, we see that in some places the surface is light in color, in others it's darker. The light areas are the **PLATEAUS**. In the plateaus, there are thousands of **CRATERS** that astronomers say were created by COLLISIONS WITH METEORS. There are also **MOUNTAIN RANGES** in these light areas. The dark areas are called **OCEANS**. 17th century astronomers thought that these were oceans like the ones here on earth. Today we know better. They are actually large, dark plains, created in eruptions when magma flowed up to the moon's surface.

PHASES OF THE MOON

We notice that the moon seems to get smaller and larger – we call this the phases of the moon. We talk about a new moon, half moon and full moon. A month is called a month because of the moon (moon = month), and in the old days, people used it to calculate time.

NOT THE EARTH'S SHADOW

The phases of the moon are not caused by the earth's shadow. When the earth obscures the moon we talk about a lunar eclipse.

THE MOON ALWAYS TURNS THE SAME SIDE TOWARD US. The other side is sometimes called the moon's dark side. That doesn't mean that it's always dark. The side facing the sun at any time is lit while the other side is dark, just as on earth. Where the sun is shining, it's daytime, and on the other side, it's nighttime. The moon also spins around itself and that means that both sides, the near side and the far side, get just as much time sunbathing.

EXPERIMENT:

Moon map. Divide a piece of paper into 30 squares and draw a circle denoting the moon in every one of them. Now color in the moon as it appears, each day for a month.

SOLAR ENERGY IN A BLACK GLASS

When the sun is shining and you're out playing, it can be better to wear light-colored clothing rather than dark. Especially if it's very hot.

BUT WHY DO YOU FEEL HOTTER IN A BLACK T-SHIRT THAN A WHITE ONE?
And why do dark objects, such as car seat belts, get so terribly hot?
LET'S DO AN EXPERIMENT!

PLEASE NOTE: This experiment may take a bit of time – it's always a good idea to have something to do while you wait.

THIS IS WHAT YOU NEED:

A WHITE PIECE OF PAPER

A THERMOMETER

TWO IDENTICAL GLASSES

TWO RUBBER BANDS

A BLACK PIECE OF PAPER

1. Wrap the white piece of paper around one of the glasses and the black piece of paper around the other one, securing them with the rubber bands.

2. Fill both glasses with water. Make sure there is an equal amount of water in each one.

3. Measure the temperature of the water, with the thermometer, and write it down.

4. Leave the glasses in a spot where the sun will shine on them for 2 – 3 hours.

5. Measure the temperature of the water in the glasses again.

WHAT IS ACTUALLY GOING ON HERE?

DARK THINGS ABSORB MORE LIGHT AND HEAT THAN LIGHT THINGS. The water in the glass wrapped in the black paper should, therefore, be hotter than the water in the other glass.

LIGHT-COLORED THINGS REFLECT LIGHT AND HEAT, which is why people wear light-colored clothes in hot countries and in the summer. It's more comfortable because you don't get as hot.

SPACE TRAVEL

The first object that was sent out into space was a Russian satellite, Sputnik 1. That was in 1957. It was visible from earth, and it emitted detectable radio waves. This was in fact all that Sputnik did, but it was the beginning of the great space race.

The first man who went into space was the Russian cosmonaut Yuri Gagarin, in April 1961.

A SMALL STEP

Eight years later, the first men landed on the moon. This was NASA's Apollo 11 expedition. On August 20, 1969, the Americans Neil Armstrong and Buzz Aldrin stepped out onto the moon's surface, while Michael Collins waited in the spacecraft.

When Armstrong stepped onto the moon – the first human to do so – he spoke these famous words: "THAT'S ONE SMALL STEP FOR MAN. ONE GIANT LEAP FOR MANKIND." What he meant was that although this was only a small, ordinary step for him to take onto the moon, it was a giant leap into the future for all mankind.

PROTECTIVE SHIELD

The rocket's nose cone ensured that the spacecraft would survive the launch without being damaged.

THE SPACECRAFT ITSELF

This small piece of gear landed on the moon and then brought the three astronauts back home safely. Incredible, but true!

THIRD STAGE

Containing fuel and gas, it first put the spacecraft into orbit around earth and then powered it toward the moon. It weighed about 130 tons.

SATURN V

The rocket that made the first trip to the moon was a Saturn V ('Saturn five'). This is the only type of rocket that has been used so far to carry people out into space, beyond earth's orbit. These types of rockets have taken 24 astronauts to the moon and brought every one of them back safely.

TALLER THAN THE STATUE OF LIBERTY

The Saturn V rocket is very big. It's about 360 feet tall, with a diameter of about 33 feet (the total height of the Statue of Liberty is 305 feet). It is also very heavy, 6.2 million pounds. That's more or less like 400 elephants! Enormous energy was needed to get it off the ground, and the fuel it used would have been enough for 800 trips around the world in a family car.

SPACE LAUNCH

The space launch is divided into three stages, after each of which a section of the rocket is jettisoned. This is because it needs the most energy at the beginning, but very little once it's reached space due to the fact that the earth's gravitational pull has very little effect on it there and there is no atmosphere in space to provide resistance.

SECOND STAGE

Also containing fuel, it weighed 530 tons and propelled the craft beyond the earth's outer atmosphere. Once the fuel had run out, this part broke away from the craft and fell to earth, landing in the ocean.

FIRST STAGE

Weighing over two thousand tons, it contained huge rocket engines and lots of fuel in order to get the craft away from the earth and up to an altitude of about 40 miles.

ME

UPSIDE-DOWN GLASS

If I put some water into a glass and turn it upside down, the water pours out. If I put a postcard on top of a glass and turn it upside down, the card falls off. But what would happen if I were to do both at the same time? WOULD I HAVE A SOAKING WET CARD AND WATER ALL OVER THE PLACE?

THIS IS WHAT YOU NEED:

A GLASS FULL TO THE BRIM WITH WATER

THICK PAPER, LIKE A CARD OR A POSTCARD

1. Place the card on top of the glass, making sure no air bubbles form beneath it.

2. Hold the card in place and turn the glass over.

3. Now let go of the card.

It's definitely **NOT** a good idea to do this in bed, over somebody who's asleep. It's probably best to do it over a sink BECAUSE, WHEN YOU DO EXPERIMENTS, IT CAN GO WRONG.

WHAT IS ACTUALLY GOING ON HERE?

If everything has gone well and you are still reading this, and not mopping up water while somebody throws this book into the garbage, then this is what happened:

THE WATER AND THE CARD STAYED IN PLACE AND DIDN'T FALL TO THE GROUND, AS YOU WOULD EXPECT, FROM THE FORCE OF GRAVITY.

This is because there was hardly any air inside the glass. We were careful to fill it to the brim and to make sure no air bubbles had formed. That meant the air pressure was higher outside the glass than inside it and it kept the card in place and the water in the glass.

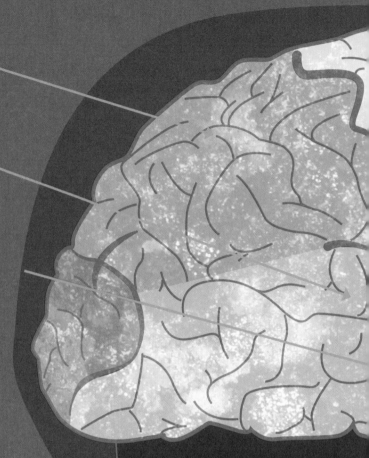

SIGHT

It may seem strange, but our eyes send what we see all the way to the back of the brain to be processed.

WORD COMPREHENSION

This is where the brain takes in the words we see or hear.

MEMORY AND EMOTION

This is where the brain keeps all the information it needs to remember: Mom's name, our phone number, and the name of the capital of Zimbabwe – it's actually our data storage!

THE BRAIN

Our brain is like an incredibly powerful **COMPUTER**. It **CONTROLS** everything we do, whether we are aware of it or not. The brain is quick at processing information. Everything we think, remember, smell or taste, touch or hear, everything we plan and speculate, happens in the brain.

The brain is terribly complicated and there is a lot about it that we don't understand.

It is, in fact, one big **PUZZLE**.

THE NERVE CENTER

The brain is the core of the NERVOUS SYSTEM. All nerves lead to it and from it. It controls our responses to stimuli.

If I touch something hot, the nerves send messages to the brain about this and it decides what to do, sending signals back to the muscles in the hand, telling them to contract so that I snatch it back. The brain does this in a very short time. An incredibly short time.

There are billions of nerve cells in the brain that send and receive information from all over the body.

SENSE OF SMELL

This is the place in the brain where we sense smell
and whether we like it or absolutely hate it.

TASKS AND ORGANIZATION

This part of the brain is in charge of handling tasks,
challenges and problems, as well as organizing things!

BEHAVIOR AND EMOTION

This is where the brain regulates our behavior
and how we deal with our emotions, whether we
are jumping with joy or screaming with anger!

BLUE   GREEN

LIKE A NUT ...

The brain is divided into two parts, the right and
left **CEREBRAL HEMISPHERES**. Each controls one
side of the body. If I want to lift my left hand the
instruction comes from the right hemisphere, and
vice versa.
This is very strange and nobody knows why it's like
this.

IN A GOOD SHELL

The brain is contained within a really good helmet,
THE SKULL. It protects the brain and makes sure
everything is in the right place. There are 22 bones
in the skull.

THE BRAIN IN A GROWN–UP PERSON WEIGHS
AROUND 3 POUNDS. ABOUT THE WEIGHT OF
THREE CANS OF BEANS.

But who controls the brain? Do we, or does it
control us? Is it perhaps really stupid to talk about
the brain and us as if they are two separate things?
Probably.
If I say DON'T THINK ABOUT APPLES! What do
you think about?

TIME TRAVEL
A THOUGHT EXPERIMENT

Some experiments are called thought experiments. They are used, for example, in philosophy and the humanities. The way they work is that you find out whether something is possible or not just by thinking about it.

Here we are going to create a **PARADOX**, which is kind of an amazing phenomenon.

This experiment is all about time travel, and whether it's possible to somehow travel backward in time.

WARNING: EXPERIMENTS LIKE THIS ARE REALLY TAXING FOR YOUR BRAIN, WHICH IS GOOD BUT CAN BE A BIT ANNOYING.

This is a famous experiment that I have simplified a little.

Imagine that you have created a time machine and that you set it to take you one hour back in time.

You enter the time machine in your room at and exit it in the same place at 11:00

You get a sledgehammer and you smash the time machine.

I know this is a bit complicated, but just read it again until you've got it completely straight.

So – at 11:00 the you that went back in time grabbed a sledgehammer and smashed the time machine, completely destroying it.

An hour later, at 12:00 you decide to go back in time but you can't because the time machine has been destroyed.

You smashed it up at eleven o'clock. Now this is the question:

HOW ON EARTH WERE YOU ABLE TO GO BACK IN TIME IN ORDER TO SMASH THE TIME MACHINE?

YOU CAN'T POSSIBLY HAVE GONE BACK IN TIME TO DESTROY THE TIME MACHINE, SO IT MUST STILL BE OK. SO YOU CAN USE IT TO GO BACK IN TIME IN ORDER TO SMASH IT, BUT AT THE SAME TIME YOU CAN'T…

So: Traveling back in time is impossible, it always has been and always will be.

I'M YOU IN AN HOUR!

~NO!!

BLACK HOLES

If we are to see things, they need to reflect light. Then we can see what they look like and what color they are. We also know that things that are massive pull at everything around them with great force. We call this force **GRAVITY**.

NOW IMAGINE A THING THAT HAS SO MUCH GRAVITY THAT IT EVEN PULLS LIGHT INTO ITSELF!

Everything gets sucked into this phenomenon, which we can't see because the light disappears into it, too.

THESE ARE BLACK HOLES AND THEY ARE OUT THERE IN SPACE.

THE MOST TERRIFYING VACUUM CLEANER IN THE WORLD

Imagine that you are vacuuming your room. If you've never done that, give it a try! A vacuum cleaner sucks up all dust and junk. You can see the small bits and pieces next to the nozzle disappear into its mouth, and the bits further away begin to move closer and closer. This is how a black hole works. It pulls everything it can reach toward itself, but rather than sucking it in, it uses gravity.

DEAD AND INVISIBLE STARS

Black holes come into being when a massive star has exhausted the fuel it burns in order to shine, and can no longer sustain itself. The pressure created by its size has the effect that the star is crushed by its own weight. It becomes smaller and smaller until the whole star has squeezed itself into a tiny dot. But it still has the same gravitational pull as it did when it was enormous.

AND THEN THEY GET BIGGER!

Once a black hole has been created, it can join with others, swallow up enormous stars, and get even bigger. In fact, everything to do with black holes is incredible. If we could watch a spacecraft being swallowed up by a black hole, to us it would look as if it was going slower and slower – but if some terribly unfortunate astronaut were on board, everything would seem normal to him. Or as normal as things are when you're getting sucked into a black hole!

The black hole would tear him and the spacecraft into pieces, right down to atoms. Then, even the atoms would get broken up into smaller pieces.

If you were to use your flashlight near a black hole, the light would BEND toward it!

WHERE ARE THEY!

They are here and there, and scientists think that in the middle of our Milky Way there is a GIGANTIC BLACK HOLE.

SHOULD WE NOW BE SCARED SILLY?

Nope, that's not necessary at all. Let's worry more about cleaning our teeth and looking out for cars before we cross the road. It's just good to know the black hole is there so we can stay away from it.

A SIMPLE COMPASS

Getting lost is kind of difficult these days. We have so many gadgets that can tell us where we are – if they work and we know how to use them. But in the old days, explorers and travelers needed other ways to know where they were. Those who didn't know ended up in one heck of a mess.

SEAFARERS USED THE STARS TO WORK OUT WHERE THEY WERE.

The Pole Star was very useful because, for those of us in the Northern Hemisphere, it's always in the north. But around the year 1100, seafarers made an important discovery. They created a compass in a barrel on board a ship. Let's make one ourselves.

THIS IS WHAT YOU NEED:

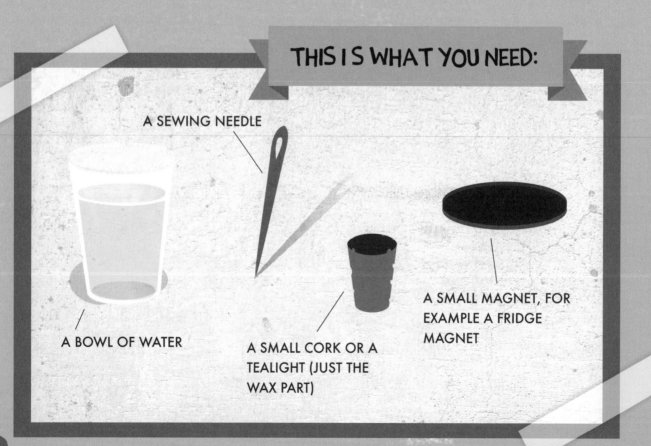

A SEWING NEEDLE

A BOWL OF WATER

A SMALL CORK OR A TEALIGHT (JUST THE WAX PART)

A SMALL MAGNET, FOR EXAMPLE A FRIDGE MAGNET

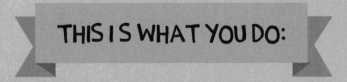

THIS IS WHAT YOU DO:

1. Holding it by the eye, rub the needle against the magnet for a minute or so. Always rub in the same direction, toward the tip; don't go back and forth.

2. Stick the needle into the cork or the tealight so that it's sticking out at both ends.

3. Put the bowl onto a table and the cork or tealight with the needle in it into the water. It should float. Make sure that the bowl is big enough so the needle doesn't touch the edges.

4. Now the needle should spin, and in the end the point will face one direction. Which is – ta da! – north!

WHAT IS ACTUALLY GOING ON HERE?

When you rubbed the needle against the magnet it became magnetized. The cork floats on water, allowing the needle to turn toward the earth's magnetic poles, and as the North Pole is closer to us than the South Pole, it will point in that direction.

ONCE YOU KNOW WHICH DIRECTION IS NORTH THEN YOU'LL KNOW THE OTHER THREE COMPASS POINTS AS WELL. WEST IS TO THE LEFT, EAST IS TO THE RIGHT AND SOUTH IS EXACTLY OPPOSITE NORTH.

GRAVITY

Before we discuss gravity I'm going to introduce you to a concept that is important to understand. MASS. So what's that?

MASS IS THE WEIGHT OF AN OBJECT REGARDLESS OF WHERE IT IS IN THE UNIVERSE.

It would be quite natural to ask: Are things not always the same weight, wherever they are in the universe? Nope – but they always have the same mass. If, for example, I had a stone weighing one pound and I put it on the sort of scale folks have in their bathrooms, then it would tell me that it weighed one pound. Good. But if I were to take the stone and the scale to the moon it would be considerably lighter, less than 3 ounces. If I were then to take it somewhere else in space, for example to Jupiter, it would be much heavier than one pound. Traveling around like that, the stone itself doesn't change, so its mass is always the same, but gravitational pull on the stone differs depending on where it is, which means that its weight varies.

This is what the scientist Isaac Newton said:

THE GRAVITATIONAL FORCE BETWEEN TWO BODIES IS PROPORTIONAL TO THE PRODUCT OF THEIR MASSES, AND INVERSELY PROPORTIONAL TO THE SQUARE OF THE DISTANCE BETWEEN THEM.

Yes, I know that was a bit complicated towards the end, but I still wanted to put it there.

THE GRAVITATIONAL PULL BETWEEN THE EARTH AND OURSELVES IS WHAT KEEPS US ON IT, AND IT HAS THE EFFECT THAT ANY FALLING OBJECT HERE ON EARTH FALLS TOWARD THE EARTH'S CENTER.

All things that have mass also have a gravitational force that pulls at other things that have mass. But the force is variable and sometimes it's very weak.

Being enormous, the sun has a huge mass. The gravitational force between it and the planets is so great that it keeps them in its orbit.
On the surface of the moon, things are six times lighter than they are on the surface of the earth. This is because the moon has less mass than the earth.

The gravitational force between the moon and the earth is what causes the ocean's tides, as we have already learned.

The gravitational force between two bodies is proportional to the product of their masses, and inversely proportional to the square of the distance between them.

The gravitational force between two bodies is proportional to the product of their masses, and inversely proportional to the square of the distance between them.

SOME FOLKS SAY THAT ISAAC NEWTON GOT THE IDEA ABOUT GRAVITATIONAL FORCE WHEN HE SAW AN APPLE FALL FROM A TREE TO THE GROUND. SOME SAY THAT THE APPLE FELL ON HIS HEAD, BUT THERE ARE OTHERS WHO SAY THAT A SCIENTIST CALLED ROBERT HOOKE CONTRIBUTED MORE TO THIS IDEA THAN NEWTON CARED TO ADMIT.

PUSH A STRAW INTO A POTATO

Using air pressure, you can surprise your friends and make them believe that you possess super strength. Well you do, actually, and it is called AIR PRESSURE.

This experiment is very simple and easy. And yet it is quite remarkable.

THIS IS WHAT YOU NEED:

A RAW POTATO

A STIFF PLASTIC DRINKING STRAW

1 Hold the straw, without covering the hole at the end, and try to jab it into the potato.
What happened? Not a lot!

— — — — — — — — — —

1 Now repeat the experiment. Only, this time, cover the hole in the straw with your thumb.
What happened now?

WHAT IS ACTUALLY GOING ON HERE?

When you covered the hole in the straw with your thumb, it should have gone much farther into the potato than before. You probably didn't manage to push it very far the first time.

By covering the hole with your thumb, you locked some air inside the straw. When you pushed it into the potato, the air got compressed, making the straw strong enough to sink deep into the potato. If you don't cover the end of the straw, the air just goes through and is no help at all.

NOW YOU CAN SHOW THIS
TO YOUR FRIENDS.
BUT DON'T POINT OUT
RIGHT AWAY THAT YOU'RE
PUTTING YOUR THUMB
OVER THE HOLE!

ELECTRICITY

There's electricity in everything. And, as we've learned, it's electricity that holds the world together! Let's try it – or at least a tiny version of it. But, don't worry, we're not going to break the world apart.

THIS IS WHAT YOU NEED:

A WOOLEN GLOVE

SODA

TWO INFLATED BALLOONS

AN ALUMINUM CAN, JUST AN ORDINARY SODA CAN

THE HAIR ON YOUR HEAD

1 Rub both balloons against the woolen glove.

2 Now bring them toward each other. Do they try to stick to each other or is something else going on?

— — — — — — — — — — — — — — — —

1 Rub one of the balloons against your hair, back and forth.

2 Lift it up gently. Now ask someone to tell you what your hairdo looks like. You could also do this in front of a mirror.

— — — — — — — — — — — — — — — —

1 Lay the soda can on its side.

2 Rub one of the balloons against your hair.

3 Now hold it close to the can, which you'll see start rolling toward the balloon.

4 Move the balloon away and make the can follow it.

WHAT IS ACTUALLY GOING ON HERE?

When you rub the balloons against your hair, or against the wool, static electricity is created. Electrons are jumping from the balloon to the other things, the can and your hair, and as they do, they pull at it.

COLORS

HERE WE CAN SEE A FUNNY THING THAT HAPPENS.

Any source of light, for example the sun, always shines every color in the world. But what we see depends on what colors those things reflect. Take this flower, for example. It reflects a yellow color but it lets all the other colors pass through. That's why we say that its color is yellow.

LIGHT

Before we start this section it would be good to get one thing straight: EVERYTHING WE SEE IS LIGHT! We don't actually see things, we see the light those things **REFLECT**. Light contains all colors, and we say a certain object is red because it absorbs all the other colors in the light, except the red one. In short, we only see things that reflect light.

BUT LET'S START AT THE BEGINNING.

WHAT IS LIGHT?

To a physicist, light is just one form of **ENERGY**. You can describe it by talking about the speed, wavelength, frequency, and strength of a **BEAM OF LIGHT**. For many years, scientists argued about whether light was waves or particles, until they found out that neither theory completely explained the behavior of light. Light is a type of electromagnetic wave that our eyes see. There is light all around us, visible as well as invisible, even if only a few things emit light. The sun is number one among those things.

Light has a **WAVELENGTH**, and there are all kinds of light, including light that we cannot see with the naked eye. For example, **INFRARED LIGHT** and **ULTRAVIOLET LIGHT** are at the opposite ends of the **COLOR SCALE**. Radio waves, microwaves, and x-rays are also electromagnetic waves, just like visible light, but our eyes can't see these rays or waves.

But we can use this light, even if we cannot see it. Scientists who work with detectives, for example, use ultraviolet light in order to see if blood has been wiped off something.

It takes light **8 MINUTES** to travel from the sun to the earth

LIGHT TRAVELS FAST AND FAR

Light travels very fast. **NOTHING WE KNOW OF TRAVELS FASTER THAN LIGHT!** This is what we call the **SPEED OF LIGHT**. In space, light travels about **186,000 MILES PER SECOND**. It takes only eight minutes for it to travel all the way from the sun to the earth, and it would take it about a second to travel from the earth to the moon.

ALL THE COLORS OF THE LIGHT

The scientist **ISAAC NEWTON** noticed that when a ray of light goes through a piece of glass, a complete rainbow appears on the other side. This happens because sunlight contains all the colors of the spectrum but each color has its own wavelength, and the time it takes the different colors to pass through the glass varies. So the light is broken up, and you see each individual color.

That's how a rainbow is created. The light is refracted when it passes through raindrops and we see all the colors of the rainbow.

SO WHAT IS A SHADOW, THEN?

We can create **SILHOUETTES** because light travels along straight lines. It doesn't flow around obstructions, like water would do. A shadow is just **NOT MUCH LIGHT**. That's why there is no need to be scared of the dark. The world is just the same in the dark, there is just less light.

Think about a box of matches. You open it and you peep into it, everything is in its place. If you close it, there is total darkness inside but, apart from that, everything is exactly as before. The darkness is just one big silhouette, so there is nothing to be scared of.

DNA

RIGHT ... NOW WE ARE GOING TO GO INSIDE LIVING CREATURES. WE'RE GOING RIGHT IN THERE. AND WE'RE GOING TO MAKE A REMARKABLE DISCOVERY

We are made of muscles and skin and all kinds of components that have been put together. The material we're made of is, actually, not particularly unusual. In fact, you could buy most of it in a store. The sort of store that sells stuff to laboratories. The only problem – and it's kind of a big problem – is to BRING US TO LIFE. And that's the MIRACLE with you and me.

WE WERE OK

When we are made, when a sperm cell and an egg cell meet up, a cell called a **ZYGOTE** is created, and it carries all the genetic information needed in order to create a new individual. It is the first thing that happens in an amazing journey that ends with us.

The zygote divides itself and turns into more cells. On and on, and the cells keep on increasing in number.
WE ARE IN FACT MADE OUT OF LOTS OF LITTLE CELLS; muscle cells, skin cells, nerve cells, and all kinds of cells. But what is it that tells the cells how they should turn out? How does a hair cell know that it should be red so that our hair

becomes red? Or how do the muscle cells know that we are supposed to be tall? How do the cells know that we are supposed to look like the best possible mixture of our biological parents?

OUR BLUEPRINT

CELLS are living creatures' smallest living structural units. All creatures are made of cells that line up in different ways and have different qualities. All cells contain a nucleus, inside which there is nucleic acid (DNA), which forms all creatures' **GENETIC MATERIAL**. DNA is made up of two threads that twine around each other, like a spiral staircase. On the spiral staircase, there are various kinds of steps that are called nucleotides. The cell can gain information from these. For the cell, this is like a diagram that tells it how to behave and what to do.

You can imagine that cells are like a hockey team, and each type of cell has a definite role. There's a goalie, defensemen, forwards, and a center, and **THE DNA THREADS** inside the cells tell them where to go and what to do.

A CELL

NUCLEUS

There is all kinds of stuff inside this tiny little cell ... there are for example chromosomes in the nucleus. The chromosomes come in different shapes and sizes, but generally they are shaped like an X, except for the Y-chromosome which is (surprise, surpise) shaped like a Y. Inside these, there is genetic material that decides how we are going to be.

A CHROMOSOME

DNA

A CELL DIVIDING ITSELF

   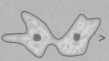

One cell   Ok, this reminds me of fried eggs!   Two cells!

PHOTOCOPYING ITSELF

Cells have different life spans. We are always renewing cells. That's why it's very important to have stuff like DNA, so that the cell can **PHOTOCOPY** itself and so the new cell turns out exactly like the older one. That's why we don't notice when cells die and others replace them.

SUPER-STRONG EGGS

Eggs are egg-shaped – of course. But why are they that shape? There are many reasons. One of these is that egg-shaped things do not roll well. So when bird mom is guarding her eggs and bumps into one of them, it's not going to roll far. Just try to put an egg on a table and make it roll..

THEIR SHAPE ALSO MAKES THEM REALLY STRONG!

I know, it's often said that eggshell is fragile, and it is; but its shape makes it possible for it to carry heavy objects.

THIS IS WHAT YOU NEED:

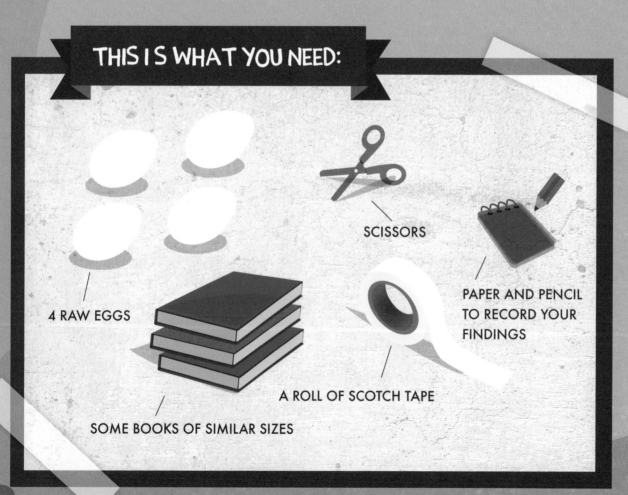

4 RAW EGGS

SOME BOOKS OF SIMILAR SIZES

A ROLL OF SCOTCH TAPE

SCISSORS

PAPER AND PENCIL TO RECORD YOUR FINDINGS

1 Break the eggs very carefully and as close to the middle as you can.

2 Pour the contents into a bowl (you can use them to make an omelet for the whole family after the experiment).

3 Rinse and dry the eggshell.

4 Now you must be very careful. Wrap some scotch tape around each half of egg, just below the break.

5 Cut the broken bits off, leaving an even edge. You should now have four well-trimmed bottom parts of eggs and four well-trimmed top parts.

6 Take the four bottoms that are rounder, arrange them in a square and put a book on top of them. Now put another book on top of the first one and keep on stacking up books until the shells break.

7 Write down how many books the shells were carrying before they broke. Now repeat this with the top parts of the eggs.

WHAT IS ACTUALLY GOING ON HERE?

Egg-shaped and convex cones can carry a great deal of weight. They spread the weight well so it doesn't all rest in the same place. That's why eggshells can carry heavy books even if they seem fragile.

THE UNIVERSE

WELL ... HERE WE GO.
THE UNIVERSE IS EVERYTHING. EVERYTHING THAT EXISTS,
AND THERE IS A LOT OF IT.

The universe is bigger than we can imagine, because it's infinite. It never stops, it's never finished. It's difficult for us to think about that – but it would probably be more difficult to imagine the opposite, that it stopped somewhere, because then we would need to be able to say what takes over from there!

IN OTHER WORDS, THE UNIVERSE IS EVERYTHING. There are lots of stars and galaxies in it. Our solar system is inside one of these galaxies. Our earth is, in fact, a tiny part of a gigantic solar system, that is a tiny part of a gigantic galaxy, that is a tiny part of a gigantic system of galaxies, that are a tiny part of the universe.

Our **SOLAR SYSTEM** is a part of a galaxy that we call **THE MILKY WAY**. There are around 200 billion (here's how to write that: 200,000,000,000) galaxies in the universe!

WE CAN SEE OUR MILKY WAY

If you're out of town, away from street lights, and gaze up into a starry night sky, it looks as if a veil is draped across it. That's where the stars are at their densest. This is our **MILKY WAY**. When we look to the side, to where there are fewer stars, we are looking into the void between galaxies. But in that void, far, far, far away, there are lots of other galaxies, except that we can't see them because they are so amazingly far away.

LIGHT THAT WENT OUT A LONG TIME AGO

The light we see from some stars is so old that the stars themselves are long since extinct and dead. BUT THEY'RE SO INCREDIBLY FAR AWAY, THAT THEIR LIGHT IS STILL TRAVELING TOWARD US. And yet, light travels faster than anything else. Let's imagine a very long conveyor belt and we're standing at the end of it. Somebody loads boxes onto the far end of it, and they move toward us. When all the boxes have been loaded and no more are being added, there are still lots of boxes on the conveyor belt on their way toward us. This is how we see the rest of the light that is on its way toward us, even though the star that sent it is no longer giving off any light.

THE MILKY WAY

SECRET CODE

MYSTERY LANGUAGES

There are many, many (something like 6,800) **LANGUAGES** that we can use to talk to each other. Some use words and others use symbols. Sometimes it's really useful if only a few people understand what you're saying, for example if you need to get a secret message to someone.

MORSE CODE
Morse code is a way of sending messages **WITHOUT USING WORDS**. You can do this by using light signals, sounds, or clicks – short ones or long ones – for each letter of the alphabet. Before all ships had cellphones and radio telephones, **TELEGRAPHISTS** used to send messages between ships and shore using Morse signals.

AN INTERESTING FACT ABOUT THE INITIAL V IN MORSE CODE
In Morse code, the letter V is represented by three short sounds and one long: dit dit dit daa. But V is also the numeral five in Roman letters. And how does Beethoven's fifth symphony begin? Da da da daaa. V was made like that in Morse code because of the beginning of the fifth symphony. You can easily find the symphony on the Internet. Just type in Beethoven 5 and listen. It's really cool.

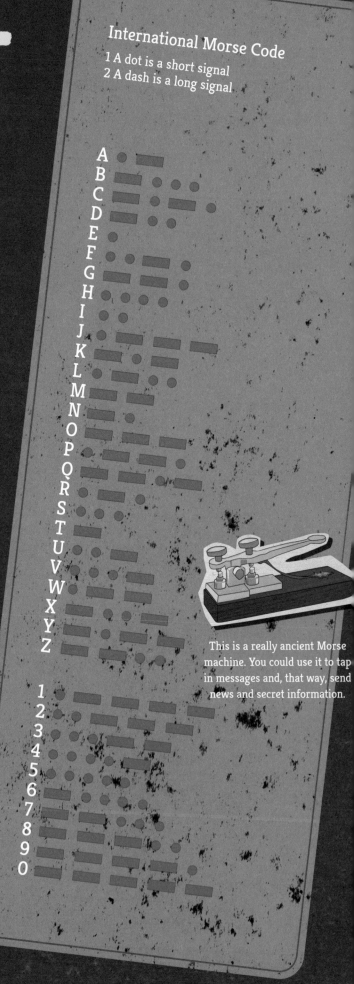

International Morse Code
1 A dot is a short signal
2 A dash is a long signal

This is a really ancient Morse machine. You could use it to tap in messages and, that way, send news and secret information.

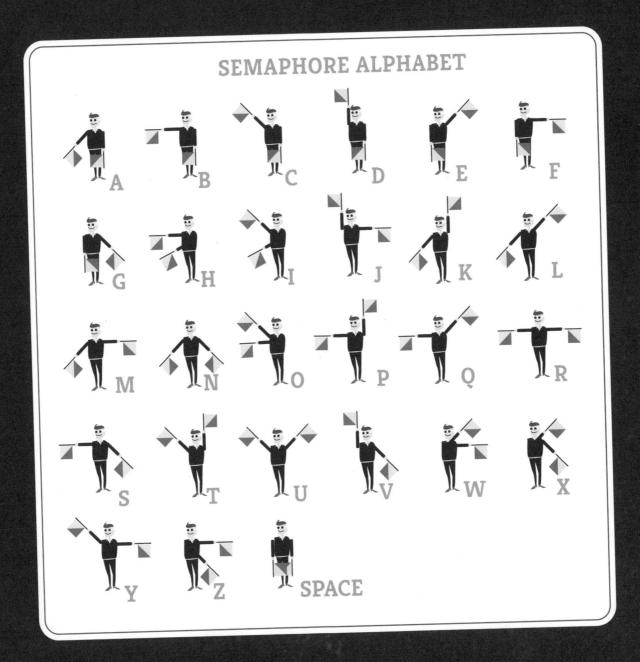

SEMAPHORE ALPHABET

SEMAPHORE

You can use semaphore to send messages to somebody where there is a lot of noise or if they're too far away for you to shout. You can also just do it with your arms, but if they're a long way off you'll need to use **FLAGS**, which are very visible.

So you have two flags, one in each hand, and you spell the words using specific arm positions for each letter. Semaphore and Morse code were not originally secret languages, but now that only a few people understand these mysterious languages, we can actually use them like a kind of secret code.

Can you work out what the Morse Code says here?

Now try to send your best friend a message in Morse code, or learn Semaphore so you can talk to each other without anybody understanding what you're saying – except of course others who know Morse code or Semaphore.

STRING TELEPHONE

Alexander Graham Bell invented the telephone. He was a remarkable fellow.
He cared about those who have difficulties hearing spoken language.
Both his wife and his mother were deaf, you see.

But nobody knows who invented the string telephone ... our next experiment.

THIS IS WHAT YOU NEED:

TWO PLASTIC CUPS (E.G. YOGURT CUPS), THE LARGER THE BETTER

ONE LARGE, SHARP NEEDLE OR A NAIL, SOMETHING THAT CAN PIERCE A HOLE IN THE CUPS

A LONG PIECE OF STRING, THE THICKER THE BETTER

TWO MATCHES

THIS IS WHAT YOU DO:

1 Empty what's in the cups by eating it or putting it into a bowl for later.

2 Wash the cups carefully and dry them.

3 Pierce a small hole in the center of the bottom of each cup.

4 Thread the string into one of the cups and tie it into a knot around the match so that it stays put.

5 Decide the distance you want between you and the person you're going to speak to. Cut the string there and thread it through the hole in the other cup and fix it the same way.

6 Now tighten the string and talk to each other. One of you speaks into a cup while the other holds the other cup to their ear to listen. Try to talk around a corner!

7 Tighten the string even more, you'll hear better. Just make sure that the string doesn't break or come away from the cups.

WHAT IS ACTUALLY GOING ON HERE?

When you speak into the cup, the sound changes into a vibration; THE STRING CARRIES THE VIBRATION OVER TO THE OTHER CUP, WHERE IT CHANGES BACK TO SOUND.

SPOOKY WATER THAT GLOWS

This water is going to become very spooky. You need a special light to see it. It's called ultraviolet light and is used a lot in discos. This is what makes white clothing and teeth become almost luminescent. You can buy light bulbs that give off ultraviolet light, and in some places, you can get small ultraviolet flashlights.

THIS IS WHAT YOU NEED:

AN ULTRAVIOLET LAMP (BLACK LIGHT)

A BOTTLE OF TONIC WATER, OR A HIGHLIGHTER PEN AND GLASS OF WATER

A DARK ROOM

CAUTION!

YOU DEFINITELY MUST NOT DRINK ANY LIQUIDS THAT ARE USED FOR EXPERIMENTS. BE CAREFUL, THIS IS SCIENCE!

THIS IS WHAT YOU DO:

1 If you're using tonic water, take it into the room and switch off the lights. Switch on the ultraviolet lamp and see what happens.

— — — — — — — — — — — —

1 If you're using a highlighter, break it, remove the piece that contains the ink and put it into a glass of water. Leave it there for a little while, then take it into a dark room and switch on the ultraviolet lamp.

WHAT IS ACTUALLY GOING ON HERE?

ULTRAVIOLET LIGHT IS INVISIBLE UNLESS IT HITS SOMETHING THAT CHANGES IT INTO A LIGHT WE CAN SEE.

Tonic water and highlighter ink contain a substance called phosphorus, which changes ultraviolet light into visible light. This is why the water glows in the dark.

THE BLACK PAGES

METAPHYSICS IS A BRANCH OF PHILOSOPHY THAT DEALS WITH THE NATURE OF REALITY. IT ADDRESSES, FOR EXAMPLE, WHAT ACTUALLY EXISTS!

DOES MATTER EXIST? Does a spirit or a soul exist? Do things like tables and teddy bears and beads exist in the same way as the atoms they are made of do?

Let's see an example: I make an airplane out of plastic modeling bricks. The bricks certainly exist, just like atoms, but is the airplane just as much of an airplane as the bricks are bricks?

Does time exist? If it exists, then what is it?

THE VITRUVIAN MAN is a drawing by the great artist and scientist **LEONARDO DA VINCI**. It's about the proportions of the human body, and is very famous. This is a slightly stylized version.

A DISGUSTING APPLE!

If I put an apple on my table, everybody can see that it's an apple. It's the same color as an apple, it smells like an apple, and it tastes like an apple. If I poke it, it feels like poking an apple. Now I'm going to cover it with a bowl.

After a few months I remove the bowl. **NOW WHAT'S ON THE TABLE?** A grey blob that smells disgusting. It's not the color of an apple, it doesn't smell like an apple, and it certainly doesn't taste like an apple, believe you me!

ARE YOU YOU??
Our cells are always dying and being replaced with new ones. At about the age of seven we have no cells left in us that we had when we were born! So we are always getting newer and newer – or what? Why not?
WHAT MAKES US US?

This is only a tiny fraction of what philosophy is dealing with, and I suggest you find out more about it. It's very useful and incredibly exciting.

And if I poke this blob it doesn't feel like poking an apple. When did the apple stop being an apple? And where did the apple go? Or if this is an apple, how can we say that an apple has to taste, smell and look like an apple, in order to be an apple?

Arrgh, my brain is bursting!

LET'S SWEEP THE MUMBO-JUMBO AWAY

If I take a broom and rip out some of its hairs, is it the same broom as before? But what if I remove a few more hairs? But what if I remove all the hairs and replace them with new ones? But what if I remove all the hairs, saw the handle off and fit a new one instead?

Where has the old broom gone, then? If I take all the pieces I removed from the broom and pile them up, does that mean that that's a broom too, even if I can't use it to sweep up things?

CAUTION!
THINK THINK

CHOCOLATE MELTS

THIS EXPERIMENT HAS A VERY POSITIVE SIDE EFFECT. YOU'LL SOON UNDERSTAND WHAT I MEAN.

It's happened to us all that chocolate has melted in our pockets or under our butts when we've sat on it, and it ALWAYS happens in the worst possible place, on an expensive chair or a couch that you really aren't supposed to mess up. But that's another story. Let's look at when chocolate stops being solid and becomes liquid.

THIS IS WHAT YOU NEED:

CHOCOLATE!
YEP, NOW YOU CAN
GO BUY CANDY IN THE
NAME OF SCIENCE (I TOLD
YOU THIS EXPERIMENT HAD
A VERY POSITIVE SIDE EFFECT).
YOU'LL NEED A FEW SAME-SIZED
PIECES, FOR EXAMPLE ONE ROW
OF A DARK CHOCOLATE BAR,
OR WHATEVER YOUR FAVORITE
CHOCOLATE IS!

PAPER AND PENCIL
TO RECORD YOUR
FINDINGS

SOME DISHES

THIS IS WHAT YOU DO:

1 Put a piece of chocolate on each dish and put the dishes in different places, for example in the sun, in a window where the sun shines, in a window that's in the shade, in the kitchen, and on top of a radiator.

2 With a page for each piece of chocolate, at the top of the page write down where each piece is. Now you're ready to keep a detailed record.

3 Every ten minutes, check all the pieces and write down the state of the chocolate. Has it started to melt, is it soft, or is nothing happening?

4 After an hour, compare your findings. What conditions made the chocolate melt? Did this happen at different speeds?

5 AND THEN … WHEN THE EXPERIMENT IS OVER YOU WILL NEED, IN THE NAME OF SCIENCE, TO TASTE ALL THE CHOCOLATE.

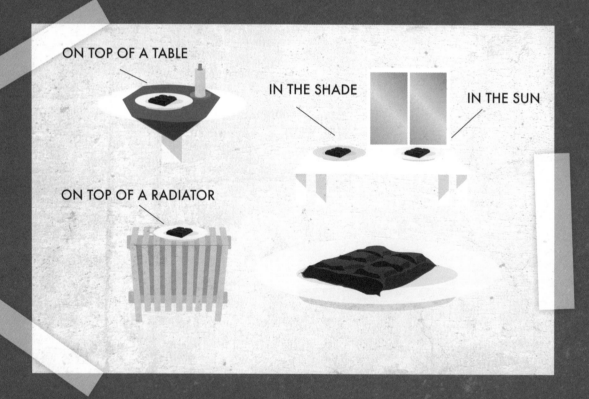

ON TOP OF A TABLE

IN THE SHADE

IN THE SUN

ON TOP OF A RADIATOR

WHAT IS ACTUALLY GOING ON HERE?

Apart from having to eat all the chocolate in the name of science, you can learn a bit from this. At a certain temperature the chocolate stops being **SOLID** (hard) and becomes **LIQUID** (or somewhere in between).

In sunshine it should melt quickly, but in shade more slowly or not at all.

COMETS

Comets are really nothing but DIRTY SNOWBALLS.

The Greek philosopher ARISTOTLE called them "stars with hair", and the name still used for them today in many languages, "comet", comes from the Greek word for "hairy". So it's fun to think that one of the beautiful marvels we see in the sky is nothing more than dirty snowballs with hair!

ICE AND DUST

Comets are made of ice, gas, and dust. Sometimes they go into orbit around the sun, just like earth and everything else in our solar system does. Some come back over and over, but others are only seen once.

THE TAIL

When a comet approaches the sun it heats up, some of the ice evaporates and the gas and dust get hotter, forming a kind of atmosphere (called a "coma") around the comet's permanent nucleus. The sun gives off powerful solar winds that blow the coma away from the comet. This creates the tail, which can become extremely long. When I say extremely, I mean EXTREMELY. It can stretch across a large part of our solar system!

A comet actually has two tails, one made of gas and the other of dust, and they always point away from the sun. So, as a comet approaches the sun, the tail is always behind it, but when it moves away from the sun, the tail is in front of it.

MAKE A DATE FOR 2061, BECAUSE THAT'S THE NEXT TIME **HALLEY'S COMET** WILL BE SEEN!

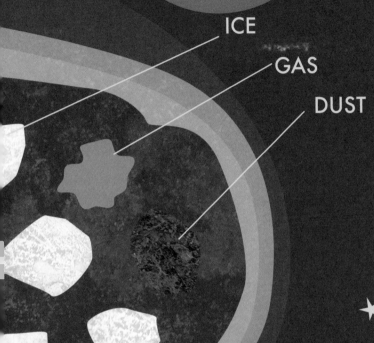

ICE

GAS

DUST

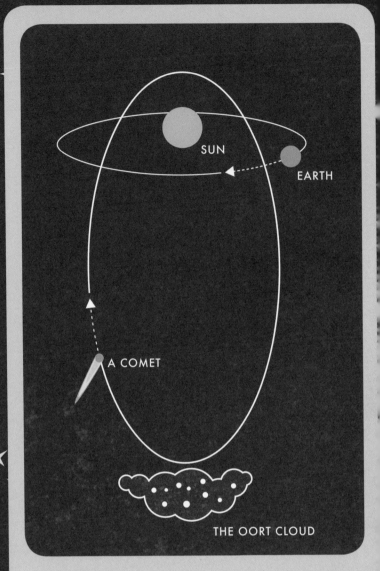

SUN

EARTH

A COMET

THE OORT CLOUD

HERE WE CAN SEE EARTH'S ORBIT AROUND THE SUN, AND THE ORBIT OF A COMET THAT HAS BROKEN OUT OF THE OORT CLOUD. THE OORT CLOUD IS A LONG, LONG, WAY FROM EARTH

WHERE DO THEY COME FROM?

Scientists think that most comets come from the Oort Cloud, which is really far away (more than 6 trillion miles from the sun – way beyond Neptune). This cloud is made of ice, dust and gas, and was created at the same time as everything else in our solar system.

Now and again, some star that's not that far away pulls at this cloud. Then the star's gravitational force pulls out loads of dust, ice and gas, and makes the snowball that now begins to be drawn toward the sun.

ARE THEY DANGEROUS?

Nope. Just beautiful. Astronomers have calculated the orbits that the comets travel on, and none of them are anywhere near the earth.

Make a date for 2061, because that's the next time Halley's comet will be seen. This showy comet can regularly be seen from earth and is named after the British astronomer Edmond Halley. It's not that big, its nucleus is only about the size of a biggish mountain, but its tail is more than 60,000 miles long.

BONES

YOU'VE GOT BONES. I'VE GOT BONES, AND EVERYBODY YOU KNOW HAS GOT BONES.

BONE AND BONE MARROW
Red blood cells are created in
the longer bones!

Creatures with bones are called VERTEBRATES. The bones keep us upright and if we didn't have them, we would be like a coat, lying in a heap on the floor. Just a blob that can't do anything. But the bones do many other things as well.

When we are born we have 270 bones in our bodies, but some of these later fuse together. Grown-ups have 206 bones.

WHAT'S INSIDE THEM?

Bones contain **MARROW**, which is where the red and the white blood cells are created. They transport oxygen around the body and defend it against bacteria.

DIFFERENT BUT ALL USEFUL

Bones are very diverse and serve different purposes. Some of them help keep us upright, we call those our endoskeleton. The **RIBS** are like armor, protecting very important organs inside us such as our heart and lungs. The **SKULL** is like a fantastically well-designed helmet around our brains.

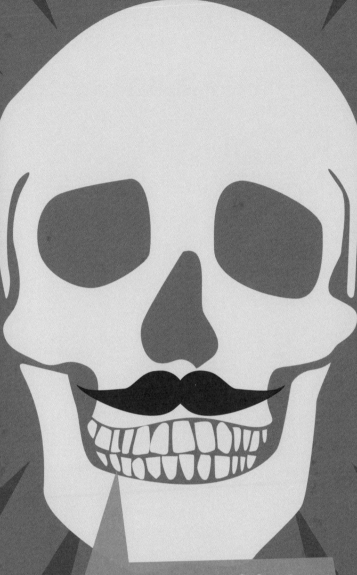

OUR TEETH ARE ALSO BONES.
THEY ARE THE ONLY BONES WE CAN SEE!

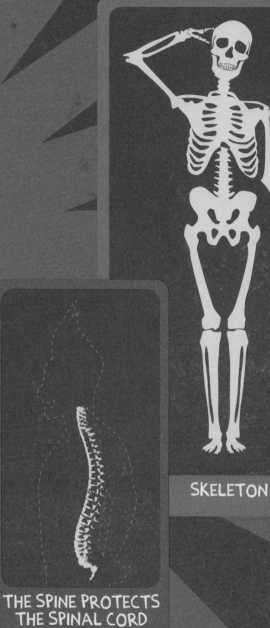

THE SPINE PROTECTS
THE SPINAL CORD

SKELETON

THE SPINE AND THE SPINAL CORD

The spine, which goes from your head down to your butt, is remarkable. It protects the **SPINAL CORD**, a bundle of nerves that run from the brain, down into the body and tell the muscles what they should do, for example when we walk.

LITTLE AND LARGE

Our three smallest bones are in the middle ear. They have Latin names, **MALLEUS** (which means "hammer"), **INCUS** ("anvil"), and **STAPES** ("stirrup"), chosen because they look like those things. The largest bone in the body is the femur, or thigh bone.

DISSOLVING SUGAR CUBES

NOW WE'RE GOING TO SEE HOW MANY SUGAR CUBES WE CAN DISSOLVE IN A GLASS OF COLD WATER AND A GLASS OF HOT WATER.

THIS IS WHAT YOU NEED:

HOT WATER IN A CLEAR GLASS (AS HOT AS IT COMES FROM THE FAUCET)

SUGAR CUBES (A GOOD NUMBER OF THEM)

COLD WATER IN A CLEAR GLASS

A SPOON TO STIR WITH

PAPER AND PENCIL TO RECORD YOUR FINDINGS

THIS IS WHAT YOU DO:

1. Make sure you've got the same amount of water in both glasses.

2. Put a sugar cube into the glass of cold water and stir until the sugar has disappeared.

3. Repeat this until the cubes have stopped dissolving and some sugar has piled up on the bottom.

4. Now, put a sugar cube into the hot water and stir until it has dissolved.

5. Continue putting new cubes into the hot water until they stop dissolving – **and remember to count them.**

WERE YOU ABLE TO PUT MORE CUBES INTO THE COLD WATER OR THE HOT WATER?

WHAT IS ACTUALLY GOING ON HERE?

I expect that fewer sugar cubes dissolved in the cold water. And why should that be? **ANOTHER WORD FOR THE WATER IN THE GLASS IS SOLUTION.** When the solution can't dissolve any more sugar, it has become what scientists call **SATURATED.** Then the sugar just falls to the bottom of the glass.

Heat is caused by the atoms and molecules in a substance speeding up, so the hot water dissolves more sugar because the molecules in the water move faster than in cold water. This means there is more space between the molecules in the hot water than in the cold, which means that there is more space for sugar molecules between them.

This is actually just like spaces in a parking lot. If the grains of sugar are cars and the water is the parking lot, there will be more spaces in the parking lot when the water is hot.

IF YOU WANT TO GET A BETTER LOOK AT HOW THE MOLECULES IN THE WATER MOVE, YOU CAN DO THIS:
Put hot water into one glass and cold water into another one as before. Now put a drop of food coloring into each glass and watch what happens. The food coloring spreads more quickly in the hot water than the cold one. That's because the molecules in the hot water move more quickly than in the cold water.

TREES

Trees are very much alive, even if we don't see them move around or eat. They can be many thousand years old and reach a height of well over three hundred feet – much taller than the Statue of Liberty! If trees could talk, they would be able to tell us incredible stories of our earth, because they've been around for so long and seen so many things – if they had eyes, which they haven't. Trees can actually tell us stories, just not with words ...

THE LUNGS OF THE EARTH

Trees are very important. Their leaves make oxygen, which we breathe. Then we exhale carbon dioxide, which they take in.

LEAVES

Sometimes we think that things are just ordinary and not particularly remarkable. Leaves are like that. We see them everywhere and we think that they are very ordinary.

But leaves are incredibly remarkable. They create oxygen, which we need in order to breathe. You see, they take in carbon dioxide and give off oxygen, exactly the opposite of what we do. Leaves use sunlight to change carbon dioxide and water into oxygen and carbohydrates, this is called: PHOTOSYNTHESIS

CARBON DIOXIDE CO_2

SUN RAYS

WATER H_2O

OXYGEN O_2

ENERGY/ CARBOHYDRATES

TREES CAN TALK

Scientists who examine trees can read all sorts of information from them, for example about the climate and the environment around the trees. **ANNUAL RINGS** in the tree trunk tell us how old the tree is, because one ring is added each year of its life. Each annual ring also tells us how much the tree grew in any particular year. If a tree grows a lot in a certain year, we know that the weather must have been good that year.

EATING WITH THEIR FEET

Trees have roots that they use to stay put and to draw nourishment from the soil. The roots can become very long and reach over a large area that we can't see without digging.

Trees drink water from the earth with their roots, the water then travels up the trunk into the branches and all the way to the leaves.

BALLOON EXPRESS

Balloons are simply amazing, and you can use them to do all kinds of neat experiments.
Scientists use them a lot to monitor the weather, releasing huge balloons high up into the sky
with all sorts of gauges and stuff to examine humidity, temperature, and winds.
But we are planning to harness the energy of a balloon and use it to drive it forward.

THIS IS WHAT YOU NEED:

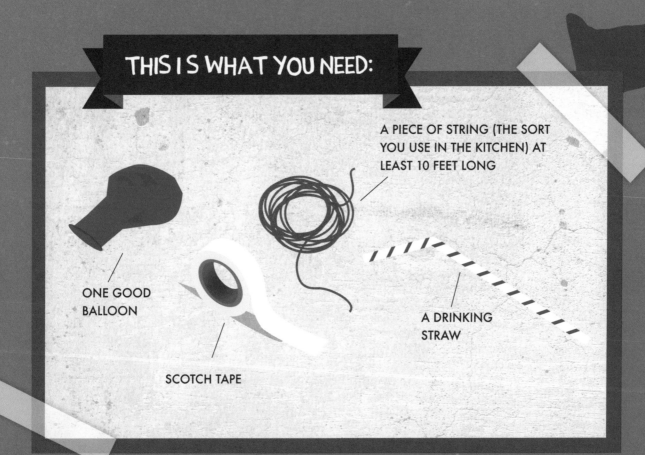

A PIECE OF STRING (THE SORT YOU USE IN THE KITCHEN) AT LEAST 10 FEET LONG

ONE GOOD BALLOON

A DRINKING STRAW

SCOTCH TAPE

THIS IS WHAT YOU DO:

1 Blow up the balloon and hold tightly onto its neck so no air can get out.

2 Point the balloon at something and let go. You didn't hit the target. The balloon went all over the place, didn't it?

3 Now take the string and thread it through the straw.

4 Blow up the balloon and fix the straw to it with the scotch tape, while making sure no air gets out. You should now have a balloon that has a straw "on its back" with the string drawn through it.

5 Slide the balloon toward you so that you are holding it and one end of the string. Ask somebody else to hold the other end of the string.

6 Let go of the balloon.

WHAT IS ACTUALLY GOING ON HERE?

By threading the string through the straw and fixing it to the balloon you created a track for it to go along. If things are to move, there has to be a force of some kind that affects them. Although nothing seems to be pushing your balloon, there is nevertheless, something driving it forwards – **AIR!** The air that is pressed out of the balloon, collides with the air outside it and pushes it away. That's why you can feel the air coming out of the balloon.

The scientist Isaac Newton came up with a law about this, we call it **NEWTON'S THIRD LAW** – the law about Action and Reaction – and this is it:

WHEN ONE BODY EXERTS A FORCE ON ANOTHER, THE SECOND BODY SIMULTANEOUSLY EXERTS A FORCE EQUAL IN MAGNITUDE AND OPPOSITE IN DIRECTION ON THE FIRST BODY.

This means that the air coming out of the balloon, pushing the air outside it (action), also experiences force from the air it pushes against (reaction), which is why the balloon moves in the opposite direction from the air that splutters out of it.

GO NEWTON!

SOUND

SOUND IS MOVEMENT. WAVES OR RIPPLES. SOMETHING GETS THEM GOING AND THEY TRAVEL THROUGH AIR, WATER OR SOLID MATERIAL.

When these waves strike the eardrum, it vibrates. The smallest bones in the body – the hammer, anvil, and stirrup bones – transmit this vibration to the cochlea, which in turn transmit the signals to the brain, which interprets them as certain sounds.

But now we're talking about hearing, which is our experience of sound.

SO WHAT IS A SOUND? WHAT IS MOVING, AND HOW?

THE EAR

It's funny to study the shape of the outer ear when you think that its role is to catch sound waves from the air and channel them into the inner ear. Many animals have their ears on the top of their heads, and they can swivel them back and forth, making it easier for them to detect distant sounds and danger in the environment.

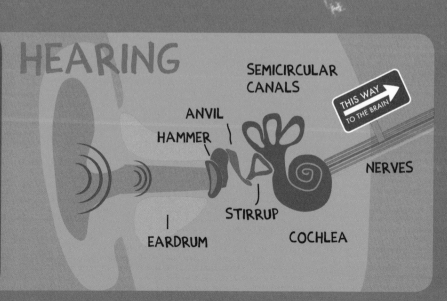

HEARING

SEMICIRCULAR CANALS

THIS WAY TO THE BRAIN

ANVIL

HAMMER

NERVES

STIRRUP

COCHLEA

EARDRUM

Vibration creates sound waves, which need some material to travel through. Just like when you create waves with a sheet, or when fans create a wave in a football stadium. If there isn't any stuff to create the waves, there won't be any sound.

It's very useful to think about a string on a guitar. It vibrates and emits soundwaves, and when they land on our ear, we hear sound.

That's why there's no sound in space. Because it's a vacuum. But we can change sound waves into electrical waves and send them into space. Then they can be changed back into sound waves. That's, for example, how radios and cell phones work.

SOUND PENETRATES DIFFERENT MATERIALS AT DIFFERENT SPEEDS. IT TRAVELS FOUR TIMES FASTER IN WATER THAN IN AIR.

There are sounds that we cannot hear, high frequency and low frequency sounds. That means the waves are either too short (high frequency sounds) or too long (low frequency sounds) for our ears to be able to detect them. And yet, lots of animals can hear these sounds and use them to communicate with each other.

A QUIET HIGH TONE

A QUIET LOW TONE

A LOUD HIGH TONE

A LOUD LOW TONE

ECHO
ECHO
ECHO

When sound waves that travel out into the air hit a hard surface, they bounce back. But as it takes a little while for sound to travel, we hear the echo a bit later than the original sound, the time delay depends on how far the sound has to travel.

BREAKING THE SOUNDBARRIER
In the picture, you can see a military aircraft breaking the sound barrier, i.e. traveling at the speed of sound. That is the speed at which sound waves travel, or about 768 miles per hour (in dry air at around 68 degrees Fahrenheit – that's important). The white cloud is formed when the air pressure drops and water molecules in the air condense around the jet.

AUTOMATIC BALLOON INFLATOR

IT'S GOOD TO USE SCIENCE TO MAKE YOUR LIFE A BIT EASIER, AND BALLOONS ARE ALWAYS FUN. THE AUTOMATIC BALLOON INFLATOR IS A REALLY GOOD TOOL AND EASY TO MAKE.

THIS IS WHAT YOU NEED:

A PLASTIC BOTTLE, FOR EXAMPLE A 20 OZ. SODA BOTTLE

JUICE OF ONE LEMON

WATER

BAKING SODA

ABOUT 3 TABLESPOONS OF WATER

1 TEASPOON BAKING SODA

A BALLOON

A DRINKING STRAW

1 START BY PULLING AND STRETCHING THE BALLOON. THAT MAKES IT EASIER TO BLOW IT UP.

2 Fill the bottle with the water.

3 Put the baking soda into the water and stir with the straw until it dissolves. There's no need to hurry here, there's nothing dangerous going on.

BUT NOW YOU NEED TO WORK FAST.

4 Pour the lemon juice into the bottle and, as quick as you can, fit the balloon over the top of it. You might need to hold it in place.

DANGER OF EXPLOSION!

DON'T WAIT TOO LONG WITH A CLOSED BOTTLE AFTER PUTTING THE LEMON JUICE IN - IT MIGHT EXPLODE!

NOW YOU HAVE YOUR OWN AUTOMATIC BALLOON INFLATOR!

WHAT IS ACTUALLY GOING ON HERE?

IF EVERYTHING WENT WELL, THE BALLOON SHOULD HAVE INFLATED AUTOMATICALLY.

When you put the lemon juice into the water with the baking soda, you were producing a chemical reaction. The baking soda is an alkali but the lemon juice is acid and when these compounds are mixed together, carbon dioxide (CO_2) is formed, and it wants to get out of the bottle. The balloon captures it and that inflates it.

If you haven't got a lemon, you can use vinegar instead of lemon and water.

SPOOKY SOAP BUBBLE

DRY ICE is amazing stuff. You don't get anything much more scientific than fog or steam spilling from a bowl and going down, not up. It's used a lot in films to make things mysterious, and everybody thinks it's cool. Which is good, because with experiments involving dry ice, kids definitely need to have an adult helping.

THIS IS WHAT YOU NEED:

DRY ICE – A FEW BLOCKS IN THE BOWL, BUT ONLY ONE IF YOU'RE USING A GLASS. WEAR GLOVES!

WATER IN A BIG BOWL OR A GLASS

SOAP

A SPOON

GLOVES

A SMALL PIECE OF CLOTH

SOAPY WATER TO MAKE THE BUBBLES (DISHWASHING LIQUID AND WATER IS GREAT!)

CAUTION!

THIS IS WHAT YOU DO:

1 Put the dry ice into the bowl and pour a bit of water over it. It'll look like a steaming witch's cauldron!

2 Immerse the cloth in the soapy water to make it soaking wet. Wipe it around the rim of the bowl and then over the liquid to cover it with a layer of soap.

3 Now watch the soap bubble get bigger.

WHAT IS ACTUALLY GOING ON HERE?

Dry ice is a kind of snow made from liquid carbon dioxide. Its temperature is about −110° F

AS THE DRY ICE WARMS, IT CHANGES INTO GAS WITHOUT GOING THROUGH A LIQUID PHASE.

Dry ice is odorless and tasteless and has many purposes. It doesn't stain clothing or furniture (just in case somebody should ask that question). Dry ice is used a lot in the theater and in the production of foods.

BLOOD

BLOOD DOES A BUNCH OF THINGS INSIDE US ...

Blood is made of plasma, red blood corpuscles, white blood corpuscles, and platelets. **THE RED CORPUSCLES** carry **OXYGEN** to all the cells of the body and carbon dioxide away from them, which we then exhale. **THE WHITE CORPUSCLES** are like the cops, they attack bad bacteria and germs that get into the body. The platelets make the blood coagulate. When we cut ourselves, they turn into a dam and close the wound so it stops bleeding. Just like when you pile up a bunch of stones in a stream to block the flow of water.

THE HEART AND CIRCULATION OF BLOOD

Blood goes around and around inside us. This is what we call BLOOD CIRCULATION. Where shall we begin to describe it? Just anywhere, because it's a circle. Let's start at the heart, or rather in the right atrium, which is the upper part on the right side of the heart.

This is where blood from all over the body comes through two large **VEINS** called the **SUPERIOR** and **INFERIOR VENAE CAVAE**. The blood here is said to be ANAEROBIC , meaning that the body has used up all its **OXYGEN** and instead it's full of **CARBON DIOXIDE**, the stuff we exhale when we breathe out.

From the right atrium the blood travels down to the right chamber (called a ventricle). From there, it is pumped into arteries, which go to the lungs. Here, the arteries get smaller and smaller, until they form a mass of tiny, tiny blood vessels surrounding millions and millions of microscopically small air-sacs.

Here, an AIR CHANGE takes place, the carbon dioxide goes out and oxygen comes in, after which the blood continues its journey, but now it's full of oxygen. The blood vessels begin to get larger and their numbers decrease.

Now the blood comes back to the heart through four large **PULMONARY VEINS**, but this time it comes into the left atrium, which is the top chamber on the left. From there, the blood flows down to the left ventricle, the chamber that's below on the left, and from there it gets pumped into the body's largest blood vessel, the **AORTA**.

The aorta then branches into smaller vessels that end up as capillaries, for example in the toes and fingers. This is how oxygenated blood is spread around the whole of the body.

Now there is another air change, the oxygen goes out and carbon dioxide comes in. The blood has become **ANAEROBIC** (just a fancy word, meaning it lacks oxygen), and it continues its journey through the capillaries, which gradually get bigger and fewer. First small veins, then larger and fewer, right until there are only two left, the superior and inferior cavae (like in the beginning).

That completes the blood's circulation.

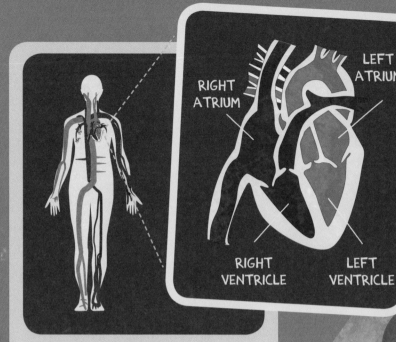

RIGHT
ATRIUM

LEFT
ATRIUM

RIGHT
VENTRICLE

LEFT
VENTRICLE

- There are three types of blood vessels: **veins, capillaries and arteries.**

- Blood is about **7% of our weight.**

- Red corpuscles are created in our **bone marrow** and live for about 120 days.

- Blood contains: plasma, red blood corpuscles, white blood corpuscles, and platelets.

- Platelets are like stones in a dam. They cause the blood to coagulate so that wounds stop bleeding.

A RED CORPUSCLE
is shaped a bit like a donut

A WHITE CORPUSCLE
is shaped a bit like a pom-pom.

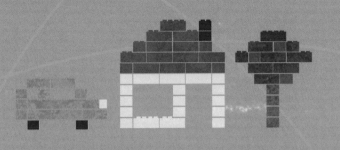

ATOMS

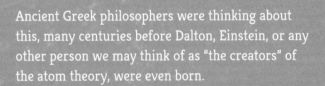

I could go on forever about atoms. They are so extraordinary. Let's start ... everything is made from mostly NOTHING! The world and we ourselves are much more nothing than something.

WE'RE A VACUUM!

Atoms are teensy-weensy and all stuff is made out of them. They are a bit like toy bricks, only much, much, much, much, much smaller, and yes, all stuff is made out of them. Just think about anything that's made out of stuff and it's made from atoms. This book, this letter, your eye, the cat next door, a leaf, the sea, the clouds, a raindrop, chocolate milk, blood, seeds, EVERYTHING..

1/10.000.000 MM

Atoms are so incredibly small that it's almost impossible to think about it. They are something like one tenth of a millionth of a millimeter. In case you don't know how big a millimeter is, take a look at this hyphen: - That's about a millimeter long, so if you can divide it up into ten million pieces then you'll know how big an atom is.

INDIVISIBLY SMALL

The British scientist **JOHN DALTON**, who was alive and kicking more than two hundred years ago, has been called the father of the modern atom theory.

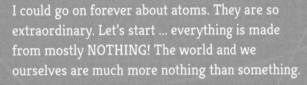

A hundred years later, **ALBERT EINSTEIN** presented mathematical proof that atoms existed. But the idea that everything was made from atoms is much older.

Ancient Greek philosophers were thinking about this, many centuries before Dalton, Einstein, or any other person we may think of as "the creators" of the atom theory, were even born.

The ancient Greeks, like Democritus (who lived about 2500 years ago), said: No thing comes from nothing, and no thing turns into nothing. Yet we see things appearing, ageing, and decaying, so what we see cannot be the stuff they're made of itself. Something smaller must exist, something we can't see. They called these things atoms (a Greek word meaning indivisible) and said they had always existed and would always exist.

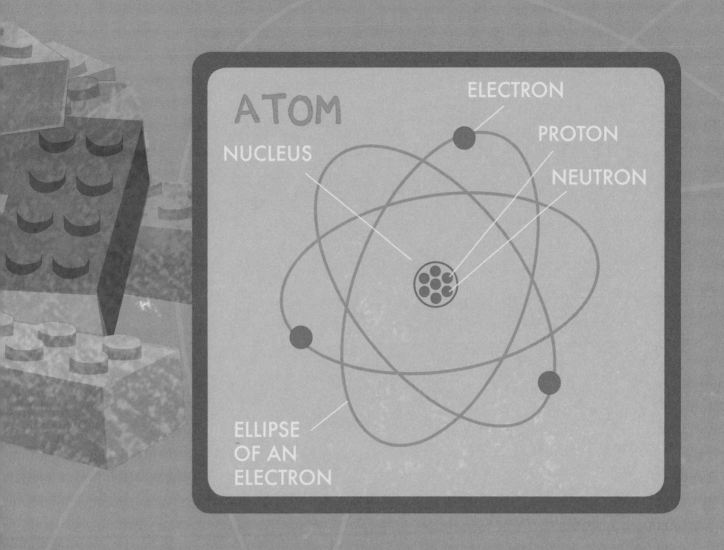

ATOM

NUCLEUS

ELECTRON

PROTON

NEUTRON

ELLIPSE
OF AN
ELECTRON

Atoms are unbelievably numerous, **COUNTLESS**, and they last a very long time. Nobody knows exactly how old they can get, but some of them last at least a few billion years. Which means that all the atoms that make up you, have already been in loads of other things before. Some of them were definitely in the dinosaurs, some in other people, some were rain, some were poisonous snakes, and some were apples or oranges. Some were all of those things!

When we die, our atoms continue and go all over the place. Just like when you take a toy car made out of plastic bricks apart and make a house, using the same bricks.

ATOM

An atom is made of three things: protons, neutrons and electrons. The protons and the neutrons form the nucleus, which the electrons revolve around. The electrons have plenty of space to move around, because each atom is mostly a vacuum. This is why we – and all things – are mainly made of **NOTHING!**

INCREDIBLE POWER

When smaller atoms fuse together to make a larger nucleus, a huge amount of power is released. We call this nuclear fusion, and this power is called **NUCLEAR ENERGY**. Nuclear power plants can generate power by splitting atoms, but the energy created in nuclear fusion is far greater. Our sun, for example, gets its energy from nuclear fusion.

ACKNOWLEDGEMENTS

When making a book like this, you can't just write any old baloney – everything has to be correct. But then you can't verify absolutely everything – for example I have no choice but to believe that the line-up of the planets is as everybody says it is, I can't check it myself.

I've relied on lots of books and websites, a whole pile of them. The main ones are, not in any particular order:

Time for Kids – Big Book of Why by John Peritano, *Time for Kids – Big Book of How* edited by Nellie Gonzalez Cutler, *How Come?* by Kathy Wollard, *The Everything Kids' Science Experiments Book* by Tom Robinson, *A Short History of Nearly Everything* by Bill Bryson, *Science* edited by Adam Hart-Davis.

... and a bunch more.

Vilhelm

INDEX

THE SUPER BOOK OF
SCIENCE